This book is
backed by
latest research
findings.

ISBN 978-0-9995575-3-2
Library of Congress
Book designed and illustrated by Stephanie Fernandez

Executive Editor Danielle Houck

Authors: Kay Lopate and Patsy Self Trand

Published independently by Pinecrest Street Company, Inc.
Address 11301 S. Dixie Hwy. Box 566684 Miami FL 33156
Printed in the United States

Researched and written by Kay Lopate, Ph.D. Patsy Self Trand, Ph.D.

THE BOOK THAT EVERY HIGH SCHOOL STUDENT SHOULD HAVE!

PINECREST STREET CO. PUBLISHING

30 Awesome

HIGH SCHOOL READING AND LEARNING STRATEGIES

THREE BONUS STRATEGIES INCLUDED!

WRITTEN BY KAY LOPATE, PH.D. PATSY SELF TRAND, PH.D.

PINECREST STREET CO. PUBLISHING

Books Published by Pinecrest Street Company, Inc.

Taking on the Challenge Series:

Making it to Graduation: Expert advice from college professors. (2017). Lopate, Kay and Trand, Patsy Self. Pinecrest Street Company, Inc.

The Official Parent Playbook: Getting your child through college. (2017) Lopate, Kay and Trand, Patsy Self. Pinecrest Street Company, Inc.

Making it in Medical School: Expert advice from college professors. (2018). Lopate, Kay and Trand, Patsy Self. Pinecrest Street Company, Inc.

Making it in Nursing School: Expert advice from college professors. (2018). Trand, Patsy Self, and Lopate, Kay. Pinecrest Street Company, Inc.

The Athletes' Playbook for College Success. (2018). Trand, Patsy Self and Lopate, Kay. Pinecrest Street Company, Inc.

Vocabulary University Professors say all College Students Should Know. (2017). Trand, Patsy Self and Lopate, Kay. Pinecrest Street Company, Inc.

College Bound Series

30 Awesome Reading and Learning Strategies for High School Students. (2018.) Trand, Patsy Self and Lopate, Kay. Pinecrest Street Company, Inc.

Become a Great Reader and Writer in College.. Book 1. (2017). Lopate, Kay and Trand, Patsy Self. Pinecrest Street Company, Inc.

Getting the Basics of Critical Thinking for College Readers and Writers. Book 2. (2018) Lopate, Kay and Trand, Patsy Self. Pinecrest Street Company, Inc.

Reading and Learning the Required College Courses in the Historical and Social Sciences. Book 3. (2017). Trand, Patsy Self and Lopate, Kay. Pinecrest Street Company, Inc.

Reading and Learning the Required College Courses in the Biological and Mathematical Sciences. Book 4 (2017). Trand, Patsy Self and Lopate, Kay. Pinecrest Street Company, Inc.

Navigating Through College Series

30 Amazing Reading and Learning Strategies for College Students. (2017). Lopate, Kay and Trand, Patsy Self. Pinecrest Street Company, Inc.

Why I Didn't Come to Class. (2018). Trand, Patsy Self and Lopate, Kay. Pinecrest Street Company, Inc.

Capturing the Experience: My Child's First Year in College. (2018) Carpenter, Sara, Lopate, Kay and Trand, Patsy Self. Pinecrest Street Company, Inc.

Capturing the Experience: My First Year in College. (2018). Carpenter, Sara, Lopate, Kay and Trand, Patsy Self. Pinecrest Street Company, Inc.

P I N E C R E S T S T R E E T C O .
P U B L I S H I N G

30 Awesome High School Reading and Learning Strategies

The book that every high school student should have!

Forward

What makes this book so awesome?

As students progress in school, we expect them to advance one grade level in reading for each year in school. We expect that by the time they graduate from high school, they will be able to comprehend college level material. This ability is important because a college education is based on reading.

When reading ability is lower than the level of the required textbook, students face serious reading comprehension difficulties which will affect their learning and course grade. In addition to comprehension shortcomings and grades, high school students rarely acquire a variety of reading and learning strategies. They are unaware that when a particular strategy is used with certain courses and assignments, learning is increased.

High school is the time when students should become familiar with using the learning strategies. Too often they prepare for their exams and classes by doing the same thing: reading and rereading their class notes and superficially reading the textbook without fully comprehending the subject matter. They fail to realize that because each assignment is different, a different strategy or plan of action is needed. Learning strategies not only guide them to completing classroom assignments, they provide the basis for improving reading comprehension which will ultimately affect a positive course grade.

In the same way a successful businessperson has detailed plans for each task, a successful high school student needs a suitable strategy for every important assignment. Simply put, as course work changes, so should the strategy. Students need to become flexible and to be prepared to pivot from one learning strategy to the next for optimal learning. This is the purpose of the book -- to equip high school students with many reading and learning strategies we have found to be successful and to show them that using the "GPS" –"Getting the Perfect Strategy" will help them find the right one to "fit" the assignment. This is what makes "Thirty Awesome Reading and Learning Strategies" so awesome--students will strengthen reading comprehension and will acquire the learning strategies that prepare them for advanced education.

Features of the strategies

Each strategy:

- Suggests courses to use with the strategy

- Describes the goal of the strategy

- Can be used individually or with groups

- Lists the materials needed

- Includes student comments

- Includes instructor comments

- States the amount of time needed to complete the strategy

- Describes in a paragraph why students need to learn the strategy

- Provides directions for "Getting Ready for the Activity"

- Provides directions for "The Activity"

- Has Home Learning "tips"

- Has "Learning Hint" (extension of strategy)

- Includes a "GPS, Getting the Perfect Strategy", which matches the purpose of the assignment with a strategy

- Includes a "Crosswalk" to match a course with a strategy

- Has a "finished product" that can be graded

We recommend that students use a strategy at least four to five times until they become proficient in using it. Although there are 30 strategies, we advise students to become competent using the strategies they selected that relate to the needs of their classes. After students use the strategy on a regular basis, they should begin to see an improvement in their test scores.

Drs. Lopate and Trand created most of these strategies to help their students with classroom assignments and exams. Except for a few traditional strategies, you will not find these amazing reading and learning strategies anywhere else!!

An added feature of this book are Three Bonus Strategies that appear at the end of the book. These strategies are designed to strengthen the area in which so many high school students need improvement. Those areas are Math, Science, and History—and, they are the usually the core courses that college freshmen face their first semester.

GPS | Getting the Perfect Strategy

Use the GPS to find the perfect strategy for each assignment!

If your textbook has a lot of illustrations	**A Picture is Worth 1000 Words, Sketch Book Journal, VTC-Visual-Text-Connection, Lock Screen, Camera Roll**
If your text has wide margins or bold headings	**Outline by Heading**
If you like using an iPhone use	**Book Bag, Say It, Then Play It, Apps for Brainiacs, Camera Roll, Lock Screen**
If you like being creative when studying	**Once Upon a Time, Quiz the Teacher, Rap**
If the material is especially boring	**Extra, Extra Know More About It, Five Minute Summary with Laptop, Once Upon a Time, Partner Reading, Say It, Then Play It**
If most of the vocabulary is new to you	**Crossword Puzzle Maker, Side by Side Glossary, Wallpaper**
If you have very little background knowledge	**Extra, Extra Know More About It, Off to the Library**
If you are going to have an essay exam	**Book Bag, Extra, Extra Know More About It**
If you are easily distracted or have a short attention span	**My To-Do List, Teach It Make A Test**

If you are working with a group or study partner	**Whiz Kid, Partner Reading, Quiz the Teacher**
If you have a lot of information to read in a short amount of time	**2 Minutes, 2 Things, Say It, Then Play It**
If the textbook is too difficult for you	**Extra, Extra, Know More About It, Say It, Then Play It, Camera Roll, Lock Screen**
If you need to study for a test	**Book Bag, Legal Cheat Sheet, Fill A Card, 20 Most Important Things, 2 Minutes, 2 Things, Wallpaper**
If you want a head start in class	**My To-Do-List, Extra, Extra Know More About It**
If you have trouble with reading comprehension	**Backup Sources, Once Upon a Time, SQ3R, Outline by Heading**
If you have trouble with organization	**My To-Do-List, Outline by Heading**
If you have trouble remembering information	**Book of Mistakes, Rap Crossword Puzzle Maker, 20 Most Important Things, Legal Cheat Sheet, Wallpaper**
If you want to impress your teacher	**Quiz the Teacher, Teach It**

Table of Contents

Curriculum Core- The required high school courses, 24 credits, for a high school diploma

CURRICULUM CORE AND STRATEGY CROSSWALK

Social Studies	English and Language Arts	Sciences
➤ Apps for Brainiacs ➤ Book of Mistakes ➤ Crossword Puzzle Maker ➤ Legal Cheat Sheet ➤ Make a Test ➤ Partner Reading ➤ Quiz the Teacher ➤ Say It, Then Play It ➤ Once Upon a Time ➤ Outline by Heading ➤ A Picture is Worth A Thousand Words ➤ SQ3R ➤ Two Minutes Two Things ➤ Whiz Kid ➤ Wall Paper	➤ Crossword Puzzle ➤ Five Minute Summary with Laptop ➤ Make a Test ➤ Off to the Library ➤ My to do List ➤ Partner Reading ➤ Say It, Then Play It	➤ Apps for Brainiacs ➤ Book Bag ➤ Book of Mistakes ➤ Camera Roll ➤ Fill a Card ➤ Lock Screen ➤ My To Do List ➤ Sketch Book Journal ➤ Once Upon a Time ➤ SQ3R ➤ Side by Side Glossary ➤ VTC Visual Text Connection ➤ Wall Paper
Physical Education & Health	**Mathematics**	**Foreign Language**
➤ Crossword Puzzle ➤ Make a Test ➤ Legal Cheat Sheet ➤ My to do List ➤ Sketch Book Journal ➤ Teach it	➤ Book of Mistakes ➤ Camera Roll ➤ Fill a Card ➤ Legal Cheat Sheet ➤ Lock Screen ➤ Once Upon a Time ➤ Teach It ➤ VTC Visual Text Connection ➤ Wall Paper	➤ Apps for Brainiacs ➤ Crossword Puzzle ➤ Once Upon a Time ➤ A Picture is Worth a Thousand Words ➤ Side by Side Glossary ➤ Say it then Play it ➤ Lock Screen ➤ Wall Paper ➤ Quiz the Teacher
Fine Arts	**Online Course**	**Career Education Courses**
➤ Book of Mistakes ➤ Fill a Card ➤ Legal Cheat Sheet ➤ Make a Test ➤ Lock Screen ➤ Once Upon a Time ➤ A Picture is Worth a Thousand Words ➤ Say it then Play it ➤ Teach it ➤ Wall Paper	➤ Off to the Library ➤ Fill a Card ➤ Five Minute Summary with Laptop ➤ Make a Test ➤ My to do List ➤ Extra, Extra Read all about It ➤ Say it, Then Play it ➤ Side by Side Glossary ➤ SQ3R ➤ Twenty Most Important Things	➤ Extra, Extra Read all about It ➤ Book Bag ➤ Curiosity ➤ My to do List ➤ Quiz the Teacher ➤ Side by Side Glossary ➤ Teach it ➤ 20 Most Important Things

Legend

Social Studies- United States History, United States Government, World History/ Civilization, Economics, Geography

English and Language Arts- English writing courses and Literature Courses

Sciences- Biology, Biology Lab, Chemistry, Chemistry Lab, Earth Science, Life Science, Physical Science, Physics,

Physical Education and Health- Physical Education, Health, ROTC

Mathematics – Discrete Mathematics, Algebra I, Geometry, Algebra II, Calculus, AP Calculus, Trigonometry, Probability and Statistics

Foreign Language – Spanish, French, German, Italian, Russian, Chinese, Japanese, Swahili, Hebrew

Art- Art History, History of Art, Art Appreciation, Music, Band

Online Courses – any subject area

Career Education Courses- these courses embrace workforce, digital literacy skills and the integration of high school course content; they are supported by school districts, local workforce boards, postsecondary institutions, and local businesses

1 | Apps for Brainiacs

Course	U.S. History, U.S. Government, World History / Civilization, Geography, Basic science, Biology, Chemistry, Physics, Discrete Mathematics, Algebra, Geometry, Trigonometry, Calculus, Probability and Statistics, Foreign Language
Goal	To increase learning by using apps
Materials needed	Smart phones, apps, textbook, class notes
Student comments	*"I never realized how many apps are available. Since I started using the "MyHomework" app, I've never missed a deadline."*
Instructor comments	*"I teach all levels of math and advise all my students to use "Wolfram Alpha", for solving their homework problems. Now they can find out how the problem was solved and I don't waste class time going over something that the students should know how to do."*
Individual or Group	Individual
Lesson duration	Time will vary.
Finished Product to be graded	3-5 minute presentation

Why do I need to learn this?

Apps are changing the way people learn, and, without a doubt, they are enhancing education. They are affordable, easy to understand, usually entertaining and motivating, and available 24/7. This strategy is a good introduction that makes students aware of useful ones for high school classes.

Getting Ready for the Activity

1. Make a list of apps you would like your students to know about.
2. The 12 apps listed below correspond to high school courses.
   Choose different apps to suit the requirements of your course.
3. Make a copy of the 12 app list for each student.

   a. Dropbox: Dropbox keeps documents safe and securely stored in one location.

   b. Evernote Peek: Evernote Peek makes flashcards for all subjects.

   c. Evernote: With Evernote students can take notes, photos, and videos and access them easily.

   d. iBooks: iBooks allow students to download thousands of books which can be carried around in a backpack.

   e. Essentials by AccelaStudy: Essentials by AccelaStudy is used to study a foreign language and includes flashcards and audio quizzes for speech and pronunciation.

   f. Easel SAT PrepLite: Easel SAT PrepLite has 75 SAT practice questions with explanations as how to arrive at the correct answer.

   g. Mathway: Mathway computes basic math, pre-algebra, algebra, linear algebra, pre-calculus, geometry, trigonometry, finite math, statistics, and chemistry problems. After it is downloaded, it does not need an internet connection.

   h. RefMe: RefMe can create bibliographies, citations, and references instantly by scanning barcodes of books and can store them in ICloud for easy access.

   i. MyHomework: My homework keeps students informed of due dates, deadlines, and managing assignments.

   j. Instapaper: Instapaper saves web pages onto a mobile phone so they can be used anytime.

k. WolframAlpha: WolframAlpha answers math questions and gives the formulas for how problems were solved. This app is useful while doing math homework because it informs the user how the correct answer was determined.

l. "I"StudiezPro: "I"StudiezPro efficiently tracks assignments and due dates for each course.

4.   Make a copy of the 12 apps list for each student.

The Activity

5.   For homework, assign each student 1 app to present to the class. If the class is large, more than one student will be assigned the same app.

6.   Each student will prepare a 3-5 minute presentation to include the purpose and benefits of the app, appropriate courses for the app, a demonstration to show how to use the app.

7.   Finished Product: 3-5 minute presentation

Home Learning

After the students have learned about the 12 apps, ask them to add one or two more apps that is relevant to the classrooms.

Learning Hint

Ask students to explore other apps and choose one to present to the class.

---

2 | Backup Sources

Course	U.S. History, U.S. Government, World History / Civilization, Geography, Basic Science, Biology, Chemistry, Physics, Discrete Mathematics, Algebra, Geometry, Trigonometry, Calculus, Probability and Statistics, Foreign Language courses, Art History, Art Appreciation, Music, Band, English Writing Courses, Literature, Health, ROTC
Goal	To learn information from additional resources
Materials needed	Additional resources such as internet, library sources, other textbooks, newspapers, and encyclopedias
Student comments	*"I couldn't learn much from the textbook—the book was on a very advanced level. Now I use an online encyclopedia and I learn just as much as the other kids."*
Instructor comments	*"'Backup Sources' encourages students to use many resources—this is a strategy that all students need to develop. This strategy shows them that if they are not learning from their textbook, there are many other resources to use."*
Lesson duration	Time will vary.
Finished product to be graded	List alternate sources, notes, and questions to be clarified

Why do I need to learn this?

There will be times when a student may have difficulty understanding the teacher and textbook. Often students with a reading level lower than their assigned textbook will not comprehend very much. As a result, the student may become frustrated and give up. Since the "bottom line" is to learn about a topic, we need to refer the student to the many other suitable references that are available. They need to know that it's OK to use an alternate or "backup" resource. Some resources available might be the internet, library books, tutoring center, your teacher, study guides from the publisher, reference librarian, and other textbooks. Remember, that since the goal is to increase understanding, it is quite possible that another writer explained the same concept in a more comprehensible way.

Getting Ready for the Activity

1. Identify the material that you do not understand.
2. Make an appointment with your teacher and the media specialist or reference librarian.
3. Find the topic on the internet.

The Activity

4. Be prepared to talk to your teacher about your concerns regarding the problems you have learning in class. Ask the teacher to recommend some alternative sources and the best way to use them.
5. Meet with the media specialist or reference librarian to locate and recommend the alternate sources related to your topic.

6. Find additional sources from the internet and print relevant articles.

7. If possible, check out several books on the subject. If you use reference material that can't be checked out, either take notes or copy relevant pages.

8. Read your alternate sources, then reread class notes, and reread your assigned textbook. Make a list of questions on concepts that need clarification.

9. If some topics are still unclear, ask questions in class, get tutoring help, or see your teacher. Let your teacher know that you followed his or her advice, show the "Back Up" resources, and ask if there is anything else that you might do to make a good grade in the class.

Home Learning

Keep your notes from alternate sources with your class notes for easy retrieval. As you study, write questions that you think the teacher might ask on the next test.

🔆 Learning Hint

Jerome Bruner, a prominent cognitive psychologist, said that everyone is capable of learning anything as long as instruction is organized appropriately and at an appropriate level. Since we are all individuals with different learning styles, we may not all learn from the same materials. In the end it really doesn't matter where you learn, it just matters that you learned it!

---

3 | Book Bag

Class	U.S. History, U.S. Government, World History/ Civilization, Geography, Basic science, Biology, Chemistry, Physics, Discrete Mathematics, Algebra, Geometry, Trigonometry, Calculus, Probability and Statistics, Foreign Language, Art History, Art Appreciation
Goal	To save time by always having study material in your book bag
Material needed	All study materials that need to be complete for homework or reviewed
Student comments	*"I listen to my recorded notes when I ride my bike to and from school. It really saves me a lot of time."*
Instructor comments	*"Students who use this strategy discover that they can learn a lot by studying 'on the run'."*
Individual or Group:	Individual
Lesson duration	Time will vary.
Finished product to be graded	Note cards, show information recorded on cell phone, and other study material in the "Book Bag".

Why do I need to learn this?

Throughout the day there will be little "snippets of time" which students can use to study and review class notes, flash cards, information on laptops, and textbooks. When students walk to classes, exercise, or wait for someone, they can take out study material from their back packs. They will be surprised to find out how much they can learn in a short amount of time.

Getting Ready for the Activity

1. Assemble class notes, handouts, note cards, cell phone, laptop, textbook, and other study material.

The Activity

2. Use information from class and textbook and make flash cards or put information on cell phone.
3. When you have small amounts of time, take out some study material from your book bag. Make this a habit. Don't waste time that might be spent studying because you will discover that you'll probably need less time to study later in the day or evening.

Home Learning

Use the "Book Bag" strategy for all classes. During the day, always have your book bag with you.

> **Learning Hint**
> Psychologists state that frequent, shorter amounts of study time are better than one long study session!

4 | Book of Mistakes

Class	U.S History, U.S. Government, World History / Civilization, Economics, Biology, Chemistry, Life Science, Physics, Foreign Language, Career Education Courses, Discrete Mathematics, Algebra, Geometry, Calculus, Trigonometry, Probability and Statistics, Art History, Art Appreciation, Online Courses, Career Education Courses
Goal	to never make the same mistake again
Material needed	all materials from which you made mistakes—old tests, questions from the textbook, returned tests, and mistakes made in class
Student comments	*"I used to tear up my old tests because all my mistakes made me depressed. Now it's not so bad because I'll never make the same mistake again!"*
Instructor comments	*"Too often we don't learn from mistakes. This is a great strategy and so simple to do. Once a week I give my students 15 minutes to review all mistakes from their 'Book of Mistakes'."*
Individual or Group	Individual
Lesson duration	Time will vary.
Finished product to be graded	Notebook titled 'Book of Mistakes containing all errors with correct answers

Why do I need to learn this?

It's always disappointing to see all the errors made on a returned test. It's even more disappointing when you made the same mistake again. The Book of Mistakes is the best way to assure that you will always know the correct answer.

Getting Ready for the Activity

1. Get a bound or spiral notebook and divide into separate sections (one section for each class).
2. Assemble old tests, returned papers, and other materials from which you made mistakes and your textbook or other resources in case you need to find the correct answer.

Activity

3. Correct all errors and rewrite question or sentence with correct information. Make sure to group all corrected mistakes according to the course.
4. Review your "Book of Mistakes" often so you will never make the same mistake again.

Home Learning

Ask a friend or family member to quiz you on your "Book on Mistakes".

> **Learning Hint**
>
> Learning is cumulative and uncorrected errors can have serious deficits for later learning. Ask students whether any of them would like to quiz their classmates from their "Book of Mistakes".

5 | Camera Roll

Course	U.S. History, U.S. Government, World , History / Civilization, Economics, Geometry, Biology, Chemistry, Life Science, Physics, Foreign Language, Career Education Courses, Discrete Mathematics, Algebra, Geometry, Calculus, Trigonometry, Probability and Statistics, Art History, Art Appreciation, Health
Goal	To learn information from photos in their textbook
Materials needed	Textbook and smart phone
Student comments	*"I never learn much from reading so "Camera Roll" helps me a lot. First I learn a lot from the pictures and then I back it up with reading parts of the textbook."*
Instructor comments	*"'Camera Roll' encourages my reluctant readers to read. They think it is fun to take pictures from the textbook. I find students willingly do this because they like anything that has do with their phone! I like it because there is so much to learn from graphic/visual information from the textbook."*
Individual or Group	Individual
Lesson duration	Time will vary
Finished product to be graded	All the photos of visual/graphic information stored in smartphone

Why do I need to learn this?

Most students seldom look at the visual/graphic material. They don't realize that often photos, charts, graphs, and drawings can convey important information more comprehensible than words.

Getting Ready for the Activity

1. Select a chapter from a textbook.
2. Tell students to bring a cell phone, textbook, and notebook to the next class.

The Activity

3. Instruct students to take a photo of each chart, graph, photo, drawing and any other visual/graphic material from the selected chapter.
4. Go to Camera Roll. Read the caption for each photo and read the section in the textbook that gives the purpose and explanation of the photo.
5. Write in the notebook (a) the purpose of each photo and (2) the important "thing" I learned from the photo.

Home Learning

For homework, review "Camera Roll" and write 1 question and answer that a teacher might ask about each photo. Collect the questions and answers from the students and give a "mock quiz" for review.

Learning Hint

Encourage students to use "Camera Roll' in all classes. Remind them that they will always have something to study since they are never without their phone!

---

6 | Crossword Puzzle Maker

Course	English Writing Courses, Literature courses, Biology, Chemistry, Life Science, Physics, Foreign Language, U.S. History, U.S. Government, World History/Civilization, Economics, Geography, Art History, Health
Goal	To learn vocabulary and terms
Materials needed	Internet, printer, and material that needs to be learned for a test
Student comments	*"Doing this strategy is a lot of fun. It sure is an easy way to learn vocabulary!"*
Instructor comments	*"Although this strategy takes a lot of time, it's worthwhile because the students think it's like playing a game."*
Individual or Group	Individual
Lesson duration	50-60 minutes
Finished product to be graded	A copy of crossword puzzle with answers

Why do I need to learn this?

"Crossword Puzzle Maker" is a clever way to learn vocabulary, terms, and facts for an upcoming test. Students will be creating their own crossword puzzles.

Getting Ready for the Activity

1. Make a list of approximately 15 – 30 vocabulary words, terms, and facts with the definitions that you need to know.

The Activity

2. Choose a free online crossword puzzle maker
3. Create your own crossword puzzle according to the online puzzle directions. You will need to write a definition for each term.
4. After you have followed the directions from the puzzle maker site, print out several copies and test yourself. Review often until all the words are known.

Home Learning

You may want to try some other puzzles and word games on puzzle sites.

Learning Hint

Use puzzle maker resources for all content areas. Use puzzle maker with a study partner.

Course	U.S. History, U.S. Government, World History / Civilization, Geography, Basic Science, Biology, Chemistry, Physics, Earth Science, Life Science, Physical Science, Discrete Mathematics, Algebra, Geometry, Trigonometry, Calculus, AP Calculus, Probability and Statistics, Foreign Language Art History, Art Appreciation, English Writing Courses, Literature, Health, Online Courses
Goal	To learn and deepen the amount of knowledge of a topic assigned in class
Materials needed	All types of reference material
Student comments	*"I learned so much more than what the teacher told us. Everything made more sense when I got the 'complete' story and not only what was in the textbook. It's good to become curious about a topic."*
Instructor comments	"Most of the time an instructor only has time to cover the surface of a subject. I want my students to become curious about what I'm teaching them. I want to learn more than just I teach in class."
Lesson duration	Time will vary.
Individual or Group	Individual
Finished product to be graded	Notes and printouts from internet to show the "extra material"

Why do I need to learn this?

Most of the time teachers just have time to teach skimming key concepts and ideas. They don't have the time to delve beyond the main points and, as a result, students may only get the "tip of the iceberg". Curious students who want to know more go "below the surface", they go below "the tip of the iceberg" because they know this extra information will make the subject more interesting.

Getting Ready for the Activity

1.   Make a list of important terms and topics from your class notes and textbook.

The Activity

2.   Use videos, internet resources, and library resources to uncover more information about each term and topic.
3.   Make notes or print out any information that you think is important
4.   Keep all additional notes and printouts with your class notes so they can be easily referred to when reviewing for an exam.

Home Learning

When studying for an exam, write summaries and include some of the extra knowledge you learned. This strategy is especially helpful when preparing for essay exams.

> ### 💡 Learning Hint
>
> Remember the saying: "The more you know, the easier it is to learn?" Being curious adds another layer or dimension to a topic. A good idea for the beginning of each course is to get several textbooks on the same subject. This reference material will provide the "depth of understanding" that may help students do well in the course.

8 | Fill A Card

Course	U.S. History, U.S. Government, World History / Civilization, Geography, Basic Science, Biology, Chemistry, Physics, Discrete Mathematics, Algebra, Geometry, Trigonometry, Calculus, Probability and Statistics, Foreign Language courses, Art History, Art Appreciation, English Writing Courses, Literature, Health, ROTC
Goal	To learn the most important information when studying for a test
Materials needed	All materials that you need to study for a test, a few 4x6 index cards, paper, pencil or pen
Student comments	*"I used to try to learn everything. 'Fill A Card' is great because when I am making the card, I am learning a lot"*
Instructor comments	*"'Fill A Card' really has students thinking about the information a lot. It's an active strategy and so simple to do."*
Individual or Group	Individual
Lesson duration	Time will vary.
Finished product to be graded	Completed "Fill A Card"

Why do I need to learn this?

Tests only sample a portion of the material that has been taught. "Fill a Card" has students making an important decision: Is this the material I should study for the test? "Fill A Card" has limited space so the student must decide if the material is worthy of being place on the card! The more that a person knows about a topic, the greater the chances the person has of predicting "what will be on the test."

Getting Ready for the Activity

1.   Gather all materials that need to be reviewed and studied for the test.

The Activity

2.   As you are studying, make a list of all items that you think might be on the test. Typically, the list is quite long and, in the beginning, all the items on the list would never fit on the card.

3.   When you are finished reviewing and making your list, go through the list and keep all the items that you still need to study and cross out the items that you already know.

4.   Begin filling both sides of the card. You may find you need to rewrite, conserving space by writing smaller.

5.   After you have filled your card, keep it with you and review often.

6.   When the test is over, ask: "Could at least 50% of the test questions be answered from the material on my card?"

Home Learning

This "easy to do strategy" can be used in all classes.

> ### Learning Hint
>
> On the day before the test, a teacher might make up a "mock review" test and let the students answer the questions using their "Fill A Card".

9 | Five Minute Summary with Laptop

Course	U.S. History, U.S. Government, World History / Civilization, Geography, Basic Science, Biology, Chemistry, Physics, Discrete Mathematics, Algebra, Geometry, Trigonometry, Calculus, Probability and Statistics, Foreign Language, Art History, Art Appreciation, Literature, Health, Online Courses
Goal	To review information immediately after it was presented in class
Materials needed	Class notes, laptop
Student comments	*"Since doing 'The Five Minute Summary with Laptop' after class, I've seen an improvement in my grade. It's so easy to do and I don't have to spend much time going over it in the evening."*
Instructor comments	*"I try to stop 5 minutes before class is over to give the students time to write a summary on their laptop--this strategy really works."*
Individual or Group	Both
Lesson duration	5-10 minutes at the end of class
Finished product to be graded	Copy of 5 minute summary.

Why do I need to learn this?

Psychologists say that the best review period should occur right after the original learning because most forgetting happens after 48 hours. The five minutes spent reviewing right after class may save hours later on.

Getting Ready for the Activity

1.   Become an active listener during class because you will be responsible to write as much as you can remember during the last five minutes of class.

The Activity

2.   Take notes as you usually do.
3.   Five minutes before class ends, use your laptop, Ipad, or other technological device and write as much information as you can remember from class without looking at your notes.
4.   At the end of five minutes, stop writing and read the summary.
5.   Keep your summaries and use them when preparing for tests.

Home Learning

Compare your summary with your actual class notes. Use all materials to predict future test questions.

Learning Hint

To improve writing summaries, read your English textbook to review summary guidelines and sample summaries.

---

10 | Legal Cheat Sheet

Course	Biology, Chemistry, Life Science, Physics, Earth Science, Physical Science, Discrete Mathematics, Algebra, Geometry, Calculus, Trigonometry, Probability and Statistics, Art History, Art Appreciation, Online Courses, ROTC, Health, Career Education Courses
Goal	To receive an A on the next test
Materials needed	All materials that you need to study for a test, paper, pencil or pen
Student comments	*"I like making 'Legal Cheat Sheets'. I keep reading them over and over."*
Teacher comments	*"I think all students should make legal cheat sheets. This is so much better than having teachers make study guides. "*
Individual or Group	Individual
Lesson duration	1-2 hours
Finished product to be graded	Copy of "Legal Cheat Sheet"

Why do I need to learn this?

A test only samples some of the material that has been taught. Students who generally make good grades always seem to have a good idea of what will be on the test. "Legal Cheat Sheet" has them select what they consider to be the essential information and write it on a sheet of paper (front and back). This "Legal Cheat Sheet" can be reviewed right up until test time!

Getting Ready for the Activity

1.   A few days before the test gather all the materials that need to be studied for the next test.
2.   Have the instructor make up a 15-20 question practice test on the material to be studied and make a copy for each student.

The Activity

3.   Begin selecting the facts and specific information that you think might be on the test.
4.   Write the selected information on the "Legal Cheat Sheet". Don't waste space writing something you already know.
5.   The day before the "real test" have the teacher pass out the 15-20 question practice test.
6.   Students may use their "Legal Cheat Sheet" to answer the questions.

Home Learning

Have a friend also make a "Legal Cheat Sheet" and share each other's information.

Learning Hint

Making a decision about what to expect on an upcoming test is a very important study skill.

---

11 | Lock Screen

Course	U.S. History, U.S. Government, World History / Civilization, Geography, Basic Science, Biology, Chemistry, Physics, Discrete Mathematics, Algebra, Geometry, Trigonometry, Calculus, Probability and Statistics, Foreign Language, Art History, Art Appreciation, English Writing Courses, Literature, Health, ROTC, Online Courses
Goal	To remember information by repeatedly seeing it on a cell phone
Materials needed	Cell phone and all material that needs to be memorized
Student comments	*"I love using 'Lock Screen' because I don't even realize I'm memorizing. It makes memorizing so easy!"*
Instructor comments	*"'After a student told me about 'Lock Screen' I gave the class an assignment—I asked them to take photos of 3 geometry formulas and use them on 'Lock Screen'. One week later I gave them a geometry quiz based on the formulas and most of the students got everything correct because they all knew the formulas--a great strategy."*
Individual or Group	Individual
Lesson Duration	Time will vary.
Finished product to be graded	Show instructor 3 photos used on "Lock Screen".

Why do I need to learn this?

Every course usually has material that must be committed to memory. Math formulas diagrams, process charts, the chemical periodic table, and vocabulary definitions are just a few examples that students will be expected to know. Every time the student uses the phone, the first thing he or she will see is the photo of the material to be memorized.

Since the average teenager uses the phone at least fifty times a day, he/she will see the photo fifty times and it will, in most cases, be memorized with a minimum amount of effort!

Getting Ready for the Activity

1. Explain to the class how "Lock Screen" will be used to memorize information.
2. Remind students to bring their cell phones and textbook to the next class.
3. Select several diagrams, vocabulary words, formulas or other material that should be memorized. In an anatomy class, an illustration of the bones, nerves, and circulatory system are examples that should be memorized.

The Activity

4. Instruct students to photograph the material that was selected (#3)
5. Go to "Camera Roll" and set one photo on the "wallpaper" screen.
6. Every time the student uses the phone, the photo will be seen and before long it will be memorized.
7. Select new photo to be on the "Lock Screen". Repeat until 3 photos have been on "Lock Screen".
8. Give a "mock test" on the materials selected to be put on "Lock Screen".

Home Learning

When reviewing, ask a family member to give you a "quiz" on the photos you used with "Lock Screen".

> **Learning Hint**
>
> Use the learning strategy "Teach It" to explain (out loud) each photo used in "Lock Screen".

12 | Make a Test

Course	U.S History, U.S. Government, World , History / Civilization, Economics, Biology, Chemistry, Life Science, Physics, Foreign Language, Career Education Courses, Discrete Mathematics, Algebra, Geometry, Calculus, Trigonometry, Probability and Statistics, Art History, Art Appreciation, Online courses, Career Education Courses
Goal	To do well on a test
Materials needed	All materials that you need to study for a test, paper, pencil or pen
Student comments	*"This is my favorite strategy. I got an A on my last test. I made 60 questions and answers. There were about 30 questions and at least 20 of them were the same ones I predicted."*
Instructor comments	*"'It's a good idea to have my students prepare 15 questions answers for homework. Then we use those questions and answers for review. It's a good active strategy and so simple to do."*
Individual or Group	Begins as an individual project and then shared with group
Lesson duration	Time will vary.
Finished product to be graded	Copy of the "mock" test

Why do I need to learn this?

"Make a Test" is an active way to study for a test. Most students prepare for tests by just looking over their notes or rereading the textbook---these are passive activities unlike "Make a Test" which keeps them engaged.

Getting Ready for the Activity

1. Gather all the materials that need to be studied for an upcoming test.

The Activity

2. Construct at least twice the number of questions and answers than the number of questions that will be on the actual test.
3. Write the questions on one side of the paper and the answers on the other side.
4. Test yourself with your "mock" test. Try to recall answers from memory before check to see if your answer is correct.

Home Learning

Ask a family member or friend to ask you the questions in a "mixed-up" order.

Learning Hint

It's always a good idea to include questions when preparing for a test. Make sure to have both factual and inferential type questions as well as short answer and essay-type questions.

---

13 | Off to the Library

Course	U.S History, U.S. Government, World History / Civilization, Economics, Biology, Chemistry, Life Science, Physics, Physical Science, Art History, Art Appreciation, Online Courses, Career Education Courses
Goal	To become familiar with the library resources from a knowledgeable resource librarian or media specialist
Materials needed	Paper, pencil or pen
Student comments	*"I am so happy I got help from the resource librarian at the public library. She directed me to sources I never thought about using before such as audio/visuals, periodicals, government publications, old newspapers, and picture files."*
Instructor comments	*"Today most students rely on the internet for research…every instructor should have some research assignments that must be done in a library."*
Individual or Group	Both
Time duration	Time will vary.
Finished product to be graded	Hand in your notes with the librarian's signature.

Why do I need to learn this?

The reference librarian or media specialist in your school library and the public library is often an underused resource person. Learning all that this person has to offer will reap benefits too numerous to mention.

Getting Ready for the Activity

1. Find the public libraries in your area along with their office hours and the times when the resource librarian or media specialist will be available.
2. Have a clear idea of the topic you need to research.

The Activity

3. Meet the resource librarian or media specialist, introduce yourself, and explain your task or assignment.
4. Take notes on the all the resources that are suggested by the resource librarian or media specialist and learn how to check them out or make copies.
5. Be sure to thank the resource librarian or media specialist for the time and information that was given to you. Show the librarian your notes and ask for a signature to verify you completed "Off to the Library".

Home Learning

High school students need to become familiar with using the library before they attend college.

> ### Learning Hint
>
> Plan an individual or group "field trip" to a public or university library where a librarian can present an overview of the library's resources.

14 | My To-Do List

Course	U.S. History, U.S. Government, World History / Civilization, Geography, Basic Science, Biology, Chemistry, Physics, Earth Science, Discrete Mathematics, Algebra, Geometry, Trigonometry, Calculus, Probability and Statistics, Foreign Language courses, Art History, Art Appreciation, Music, Band, English Writing Courses, Literature, Health, ROTC
Goal	To make sure all assignments and obligations are completed.
Materials needed	Paper, pencil, pen, and school planner
Student comments	*"Now I never forget anything. Now I'm much better organized and I like getting everything done on time. I make a to-do list every day.*
Instructor comments	*"Making a To-Do List is the habit all students should acquire."*
Individual or Group	Individual
Lesson duration	5-10 minutes daily
Finished product to be graded	Make a copy of all "To Do Lists" and show these and planner to instructor

Why do I need to learn this?

Most high school students have many responsibilities. Forgetting to do some of them could have serious consequences. A "To-Do" list will help students stay focused on their studies and not on routine responsibilities.

33

Getting Ready for the Activity

1. Get paper, pencil, pen, and monthly planner together.

Activity

2. Decide whether your "To-Do List" will be a weekly or daily list.
3. Weekly "To-Do List": Consult your school planner that has all important due dates, test dates, meetings, practices, social events, birthdays, anniversaries, bills to be paid, work schedule, and anything else that needs to be accomplished that week. Transfer these dates to the weekly "To-Do List".
    Daily "To-Do List": In the evening or in the morning consult your school planner and other sources and write down all the important tasks that you hope to accomplish in one day.
4. Keep your "To-Do List" nearby and when the item has been complete, check it off.

Home Learning

Use a small, separate notebook for your "To-Do Lists".

Learning Hint

"To-Do Lists" help you stay organized and "on top of" all your responsibilities.

---

15 | Once Upon A Time

Course	U.S History, U.S. Government, World , History / Civilization, Economics, Biology, Chemistry, Life Science, Earth Science, Physical Science, Physics, Foreign Language, Career Education Courses, Art History, Art Appreciation
Goal	To remember information that has been rewritten into a story
Materials needed	Textbook, paper, pencil or pen
Student comments	*"It's so much easier to remember a story. I like using my imagination and all my classmates like my stories!"*
Instructor comments	*"We tried this strategy in a biology class. It was a lesson about how phagocytes destroy germs. The students were so imaginative and their stories were great. I'm going to do this strategy again."*
Individual or group	Begins as an individual project and then shared with a group.
Lesson duration	Time will vary.
Finished product to be graded	Make a copy of "Once Upon a Time" story

Why do I need to learn this?

It's always easier to remember a story than trying to remember textbook information. This strategy can turn a dull subject into an interesting and entertaining story.

"If history were taught in the form of stories, it would never be forgotten."
Rudyard Kipling

Getting Ready for the Activity

1.   Choose a textbook reading assignment.

The Activity

2.   Read the selection.
3.   Turn the selection into a story by saying,
        Once upon a time, there……"
4.   An example of this strategy is given below. Several pages in a geography
        textbook described "The Black Triangle". Below is the story that a student
        wrote after reading about it in the textbook.
5.   Read the story you created from your textbook reading assignment several
        times before the test.

"Once upon a time the forests in Germany, Poland, and the Czech Republic were
beautiful and free of pollution. Mr. and Mrs. Novak loved the beautiful forests,
lakes, rivers, trees, plants, and animals. Every Sunday the Novaks and their
daughters had picnics in the countryside. Then a terrible thing happened. The
Communists took over and built mines, coal powered power plants, factories
that produced toxic pollutants and poisons that destroyed the atmosphere, rivers,
lakes, and land. The forests became industrial centers. The most severe area
destroyed was called The Black Triangle which included the Sudety Mountains
of the Czech Republic. Acid rain and heavy metals such as mercury, lead,
coalmines salts, and organic carcinogens can still be found in the region today
but, thanks to United Nations Economic Commission for Europe, there have been
massive efforts to restore the land. Mr. and Mrs. Novak became ill while in their
late 40's and died a few years later. Their early death was the result of pollution.
Their daughters are members of an active health committee whose goal is to
restore a new triangle---the Green Triangle.

Home Learning

After you have made a few "stories" from your textbook, read them to a friend or family member. On the next day, ask them to repeat the story. You will find that they probably remembered most of the story.

> -💡- **Learning Hint**
>
> If you have a creative mind or a lively imagination, you will enjoy this strategy.

You're on your way to becoming an **amazing** student!

16 | Outline by Heading

Course	U.S. History, U.S. Government, World History / Civilization, Geography, Basic Science, Biology, Chemistry, Physics, Foreign Language, Art History, Art Appreciation, Literature, Health, ROTC, Online Courses, Career Education Courses
Goal	To learn information in an organized, structured way
Materials needed	textbook, paper, pencil or pen
Student comments	*"I used to highlight my textbook. I never thought about doing anything else until I learned this strategy. It's good when the teacher says 'know everything in the chapter.'"*
Instructor comments	*"This is a good textbook notetaking strategy. It takes a lot of time but the students really learn the information,*
Individual or Group	Individual
Lesson duration	Time will vary.
Finished product to be graded	Make a copy of completed "Outline by Heading"

Why do I need to learn this?

Textbook information that is organized with many headings is easier to understand than continuous text (without headings) that may extend over several pages. "Outline by Heading" instructs the reader to read from heading to heading and then to write a summary of what was just read.

Getting Ready for the Activity

1. Choose a section of a chapter which has many major, minor and sub-headings.
2. Copy the headings on a piece of paper. Make sure you leave 2-3 lines between the headings and indent according to the level of the heading.

The Activity

3. Read the textbook starting from the first heading to the next heading.
4. Think about what you just read and write some important facts and details in the space between the headings.
5. Continue until you have some facts and details between each heading.
6. Use your completed "Outline by Heading" for review.

Home Learning

Use "Outline by Heading" for all reading material which has many headings. You will never get bored or sleepy using this strategy because you are actively involved with writing. Get into the habit of using this strategy when you want a high degree of comprehension.

Learning Hint

Have you ever tried to learn a lot of random facts? When facts and details are grouped or organized, it becomes easy to "see" how they "fit" into the overall concept. The outstanding feature of "Outline by Heading" is that the facts and details are grouped under the heading to which they belong. Remember, information that is learned in an organized way is the "key to a powerful long-term memory".

17 | Partner Reading

Course	U.S History, U.S. Government, World , History / Civilization, Economics, Biology, Chemistry, Life Science, Earth Science, Physical Science, Physics, Literature courses, Foreign Language, Online Courses
Goal	To improve reading comprehension with a partner
Materials needed	Textbook, timer, paper, pencil or pen
Student comments	*"I like reading with someone."*
Instructor comments	*"Partner Reading is easy to do and the kids really like it. They take turns reading orally and then answer their partner's questions."*
Individual or Group	Groups: 2 students in a group
Lesson duration	Time will vary.
Finished product to be graded	Make a copy of the 6 questions and answers

Why do I need to learn this?

"Partner Reading" is an active reading strategy which has students reading aloud—a nice change from silent reading. Comprehension is monitored because each partner is asked questions on what was read. The strategy includes reading comprehension, listening, and cooperative learning.

Getting Ready for the Strategy

1. Select a section from a science, social studies, geography, history, or health book.
2. Group students into groups of two. Make sure each group member has his/her textbook and paper and pencil.

The Activity

3. The first group member reads aloud for three minutes. (It's OK to give a little more time to finish a paragraph.) While the first member is reading, the second member writes 2 questions and answers based on Group one's information. (The second group member is also responsible to keep track of time.)
4. Now the second group member reads aloud for three minutes or longer until the end of a paragraph. While the second group member is reading, the first group member writes two questions and answers on the information the first group member just read.
5. Repeat #3-4 two more times until each group member has read three times and has written six questions and answers.
6. Each group member takes turns asking the questions to his/her partner. If necessary, verify answers in the textbook.

18 | A Picture Is Worth 1000 Words

Course	U.S History, U.S. Government, World, History/ Civilization, Economics, Biology, Chemistry, Life Science, Physics, Physical Science, Life Science, Earth Science, Art History, Art Appreciation
Goal	To improve comprehension by understanding visual/graphic material
Materials needed	Textbook, paper, pencil or pen
Student comments	*"I never used to take the time to look at the pictures, charts, graphs, and drawings in my books. It's worth it to spend a little time trying to understand them."*
Instructor comments	*"Visual material is included in textbooks to increase understanding because sometimes a picture can explain something better than words."*
Lesson duration	Approximately 8-10 minutes per illustration
Individual or Group	Individual
Finished product to be graded	Submit the purpose, main idea, and 2 questions and answers for each drawing, illustration, chart, graph, cartoon, and other visual display in the chapter.

Why do I need to learn this?

Spending a few minutes to understand the purpose and main idea of an illustration, graph, cartoon, chart, map, or other visual displays is an excellent strategic plan. "A Picture is Worth 1000 Words" will give a solid base when the student begins reading the text.

Getting Ready for the Activity

1.   Select a chapter that needs to be read for an upcoming test.

The Activity

2.   Scan the pages in the chapter and stop at each drawing, illustration, chart, graph, cartoon, and other visual display.
3.   Read the title and caption.
4.   Spend 1-2 minutes studying the visual/graphic display and write the purpose, main idea, and 2 questions (and answers) that a teacher might ask.
5.   Complete #3-4 until there is a main idea and 2 questions and answers for each visual/graphic display.

Home Learning

Understanding the purpose and main idea of visual material should reduce the amount of time it usually takes to read a chapter. Students should practice this strategy with reading materials found in the home.

> ### Learning Hint
>
> This strategy builds a strong foundation to foster comprehension. Previewing the visual material before reading gives the reader a definite advantage.

19 | Quiz the Teacher

Course	U.S History, U.S. Government, World , History/ Civilization, Economics, Biology, Chemistry, Life Science, Physics, Foreign Language, Career Education Courses, Career Education Courses, Foreign Language
Goal	To learn information by "switching roles"
Materials needed	All materials that you need to study for a test, a few 4x6 index cards, paper, pencil or pen
Student comments	*"I like quizzing my teacher and she gets very embarrassed when she can't answer a question!"*
Instructor comments	*"This is fun to do but I have to study the material thoroughly because the students always ask difficult questions."*
Individual or Group	Group
Lesson duration	Time will vary.
Finished product to be graded	Submit 10 questions and the answers given by the teacher

Why do I need to learn this?

"Quiz the Teacher" is entertaining and everyone has a good time! It's fun to "switch roles" and let the students ask the questions to the teacher instead of always having to answer questions given by the teacher.

Getting Ready for the Activity

1. Select a chapter in textbook.
2. Select a scorekeeper.

The Activity

3. Day 1: Tell the students they have 20 minutes to read the chapter and write 10 questions and answers on a separate piece of paper. The questions should be short answer such as true/false, definition, or factual. They are to finish the assignment as homework.
4. Day 2: Students take out their questions and take turns asking one question to the teacher. The student asking the question will determine if the teacher's answer is correct.
5. The scorekeeper keeps track of the teacher's correct and incorrect answers.
6. If a question has already been asked, it cannot be asked again so the student must ask a different question.
7. When all the questions have been asked and answered, the scorekeeper tells the class the percentage correct earned by the teacher.

Home Learning

Making questions is an active strategy that keeps students engaged in the task. When homework or other assignments are completed, a habit students should acquire is to use the information and generate a few questions they think that a teacher might ask.

Learning Hint

It makes sense that if questions are used to assess student learning, then questions should be used when reviewing and studying.

20 | Rap

Course	U.S. History, U.S. Government, World History / Civilization, Geography, Basic Science, Biology, Chemistry, Physics, Discrete Mathematics, Algebra, Geometry, Trigonometry, Calculus, Probability and Statistics, Foreign Language, Art History, Art Appreciation, Music, Band, English Writing Courses, Literature, Health, Career Education Courses
Goal	To help remember concepts, main ideas, supporting details, and vocabulary by creating a poem or rap.
Materials needed	All materials that need to be reviewed for a test
Student comments	*"At first I didn't want to do this but now I usually do one poem for every major test. This strategy is a lot of fun."*
Instructor comments	*"In a last review session several students read their "Rap/ Poems"--they were very clever and all the students said they learned a lot from hearing them."*
Individual or Group	Begins as an individual activity but the "rap" should be shared with the group
Lesson duration	Time will vary.
Finished product to be graded	Submit "Rap" or poem

Why do I need to learn this?

Tests usually cover a lot of information that must be remembered. "Rap" is a lot of fun, it gives the students a chance to be creative, and it is easy for them to remember a "catchy" poem or rap.

Getting Ready for the Activity

1.   Before the next test, select material that needs to be learned. Include class notes, handouts, and textbook chapters.

The Activity

2.   Begin the poem or rap by selecting the main idea (The title is often the main idea).
3.   Add supporting details and important terms and vocabulary.
4.   Add "powerful", vibrant adjectives and verbs to make your poem or rap memorable.
5.   Try to make your poem or rap "rhyme and click".
6.   Edit your poem or rap and make sure it includes all the main ideas, supporting details, and vocabulary you need to learn for the test.
7.   Write your final draft.
8.   Share your poem with classmates.
9.   Recite your poem many times before the test.

Home Learning

Write another poem from a different section or chapter. Consult a rhyming dictionary for added impact!

Learning Hint

Share poems to your classmates. Their poems will help you remember.

---

21 | Say It, Then Play It

Course	U.S History, U.S. Government, World , History/ Civilization, Economics, Biology, Chemistry, Life Science, Physics, Physical Science, Earth Science, Foreign Language, Online Courses, Foreign Language, Music
Goal	To learn information from listening.
Materials needed	Textbook, class notes, smartphone
Student comments	*"I learn a lot more listening than reading. It's so simple to do and I keep all my recordings in my book bag so I always have something to study."*
Instructor comments	*"'Say It, Then Play It' is effective because students are using their visual and auditory modes.'"*
Individual or Group	Individual
Lesson duration	Time will vary.
Finished product to be graded	Either send your instructor the recordings or show your instructor how used your smart phone to record text information.

Why do I need to learn this?

Do your eyes become tired after a two hour study session? Do you ever get bored reading chapter after chapter? "Say It, Then Play It" is a strategy that you can do while driving, exercising, or lying in bed. It is especially good for auditory learners and for anyone who needs a little variety in studying.

Getting Ready for the Activity

1. Select material that needs reviewing for an upcoming test.
2. Obtain a smartphone

The Activity

3. Begin reading your class notes into the smartphone.
4. Find corresponding information from the textbook and read that information into the smartphone.
5. Listen to the recordings.

Home Learning

Preview the next chapter by reading at least 3-4 pages into the smartphone. Listen to recording before the teacher explains it in class the next day.

Learning Hint

Often reading is the only strategy students use. Although most students are visual learners, every student will benefit when the listening modality is added because both sides of the brain are involved. The technology available today makes "Say It, Then Play It" easy to use.

22 | Side by Side Glossary

Course	U.S History, U.S. Government, World , History / Civilization, Economics, Biology, Chemistry, Earth Science, Life Science, Physical Science, Physics, Foreign Language, Online Courses, Health
Goal	To learn the new terms in the chapter
Materials needed	Textbook with glossary, stapler, colored markers, pencil or pen
Student comments	*"Now it's easy to remember the new terms and vocabulary. I use it for my history class and I did very well on my last test."*
Instructor comments	*"I require my students to use this strategy. In all my years of teaching, I think this strategy is my favorite. I use it in social studies but it can be used in any course that has a textbook with a glossary."*
Individual or group	Individual
Lesson duration	Time will vary.
Finished product to be graded	Show your instructor your "Side by Side Glossary".

Why do I need to learn this?

Since vocabulary contributes so much to reading comprehension, it is essential to learn all the new terms, vocabulary, names, and events in a chapter. Unfortunately, students don't refer to the glossary as much as they should. Another valuable feature of the "Side by Side Glossary" is that it provides several encounters with the new term.

Getting Ready for the Activity

1. Make a copy of the glossary and staple it together.

The Activity

2. Begin reading the chapter and highlight each new term. (All the words in each chapter are highlighted in the same color.)
3. Find the same term in the glossary and highlight the term and definition the same color.
4. Read the term's glossary definition and also the term as it appears in the text.
5. Complete reading the chapter and continue highlighting each term as written in context and also as written in the glossary.
6. Use your color-coded glossary for review.
7. Continue using this strategy with the next chapter. Remember to use a different color marker for each chapter.

Home Learning

Ask a family member or classmate to give you a "quiz" using your color-coded glossary.

> **Learning Hint**
>
> The words in the "Side by Side" glossary are color coded according to chapter. When learning new words, it is always advantageous to have them grouped according to the chapter's topic.

23 | Sketch Book Journal

Course	Biology, Chemistry, Earth Science, Life Science, Physical Science, Physics, Physical Education, Health, ROTC, Art History, Art Appreciation, Online Courses
Goal	To remember information by drawing or sketching
Materials needed	Sketch pad or separate notebook, textbook, class notes, paper, colored pens and pencils.
Student comments	*"I started making a 'Sketch Book Journal' for biology and since then I am getting high grades like the strategy and I like that the sketches are altogether in one journal."*
Instructor comments	*"'This is an excellent strategy because making your own sketch is so much better than looking at one from textbook."*
Individual or group	Begins as an individual project but students should be encouraged to show their sketches to the group.
Lesson duration	Approximately 10-15 minutes per sketch
Finished product to be graded	Show your instructor your "Sketch Book Journal".

Why do I need to learn this?

It's much easier to remember a picture you have seen rather than remembering a written paragraph. It is even easier to remember the picture if you drew it yourself. Drawing your own sketches in your "Sketch Book Journal" is not only an excellent strategy for retaining information but it is also fun to do!

Getting Ready for the Activity

1. Choose a textbook from a class that has many diagrams, charts, graphs, and other visual information.
2. Get colored pencils, pens and a sketch pad or separate notebook and label it "My Sketch Book Journal."

The Activity

3. Refer to the textbook drawings but sketch your own You may also read about concepts and then turn the written explanation into your own diagram, chart, graph, or other visual/graphic drawing.
4. Label all parts of each sketch. Also include the topic, date, page number, and chapter.
5. Make sure your sketches are colorful.
6. Write a brief description for each sketch. Explain it in your own words.

Home Learning
Study your "Sketch Book Journal" drawings for the next exam.

Learning Hint

Use other sources for visual/graphic drawings.

---

24 | SQ3R

Course	U.S History, U.S. Government, World , History/ Civilization, Economics, Biology, Chemistry, Life Science, Physics, Online courses, Health, Art History, Art Appreciation, Health, Online Courses
Goal	To learn the textbook information
Materials needed	Textbook, highlighters, paper, pencil or pen
Student comments	*"It's a lot of work and takes a lot of time but I really learned and got an A on my test."*
Instructor comments	*"'SQ3R is a 'tried and true' learning strategy. I especially like the 'recite' stage.*
Individual or group	Individual
Lesson duration	45-60 minutes
Finished product to be graded	Show your instructor the textbook chapter with headings turned to questions and the highlighting in the text which answer the questions.

Why do I need to learn this?

The steps in SQ3R--- Survey, Question, Read, Recite and Review contain the all-important components for reading comprehension. Most reading professionals consider SQ3R is the most fundamental reading comprehension strategy.

Getting Ready for the Activity

1.   Select a chapter from a textbook.

The Activity

2.   <u>Survey:</u> Begin building knowledge about the chapter before you begin to read.

   <u>a.</u> Read the title and introductory paragraph(s). Usually the title and introduction give the background of the topic and a summary of what is to be learned and the purpose of why you should learn the information.

   <u>b.</u> After reading the introduction, read the all headings, subheadings and italicized words in the chapter. This will give you a conceptualized outline of the information throughout the chapter.

   <u>c.</u> Finally, read the summary at the end of the chapter. If your chapter does not have a summary, read the last paragraph at the end of each heading section.

3.   <u>Question:</u> With a pencil or pen, turn the first heading into a question. Formulate your question using when, why, where, what and how. You should be able to write a good strong question because of the prior knowledge you built in the survey section. Keep in mind the quiz or test questions you may get from your teacher—try to mimic the kind of questions your teacher asks.

4.   <u>Read:</u> Now read for the answer to the question. Highlight the answer to the question. If you feel you want to highlight other information, highlight it in a different color.

5.   <u>Recite:</u> Before reading the next section, close the book and try to recite all the information in the section you just rea. Make sure you can recite the answer to your question. Remember, this might be a test question. Continue reading each section using steps 3-5 (question, read, and recite).

6.   <u>Review:</u> Go through all of the heading questions and see if you can answer all of the questions without the aid of the book. Make sure you can fully answer the questions by telling yourself the concepts, main points, and sub points.

Home Learning

Use SQ3R in all your content courses. Remember to make mock tests!

- Learning Hint

Listed below are question word prompts to help you formulate your questions.

Define	Describe	Label	List	Name
Outline	Reproduce	Select	State	Convert
Distinguish	Estimate	Explain	Generate	Paraphrase
Calculate	Examine	Classify	Relate	Interpret
Differentiate	Breakdown	Infer	Rank	Solve
Predict	Create	Compose	Design	Develop
Assess	Critique	Evaluate	Judge	Justify

---

25 | Teach It

Course	U.S History, U.S. Government, World , History/ Civilization, Economics, Biology, Chemistry, Earth Science, Life Science, Physical Science, Physics, Foreign Language, Career Education Courses, Discrete Mathematics, Algebra Geometry, Calculus, Trigonometry, Probability and Statistics, Art History, Art Appreciation, Music, Band, Online Courses, Career Education Courses, Physical Education, Health, ROTC
Goal	To learn important information by teaching it
Materials needed	All materials that you need to study for a test, paper, pencil or pen
Student comments	*"I like using 'Teach It' because it gives me a chance to explain what I learned to someone. I like using my whiteboard because it makes me feel more like a teacher."*
Instructor comments	*"It's true that 'we learn by doing' and that we can learn a lot by teaching or explaining the information to someone else."*
Individual or Group	Begins as an individual project and then becomes a group activity
Lesson duration	40-60 minutes
Finished product to be graded	Submit your lesson plans for the 10-20 minute lesson you "gave" to your classmates.

Why do I need to learn this?

One of the best ways to learn something is to teach it to someone else. Students like taking the part of the teacher. They prepare a lesson and then "teach it". This strategy involves selecting the material to teach, writing about it, and delivering it. It is an active strategy including reading, writing, and speaking.

Getting Ready for the Activity

1. Assemble class notes and corresponding material from the textbook.

The Activity

2. Create a 10-20 minute lesson and "give" your lesson to your class, a family member or friend.

Home Learning

In the evening, "Teach It" is an active way to review the material taught that day. Reinforce the learning by using a whiteboard and colored markers.

> ### Learning Hint
>
> The best way to maximize learning is to "Teach It". Assign students different topics to teach their classmates.

26 | Twenty Most Important Things

Course	U.S History, U.S. Government, World , History / Civilization, Economics, Biology, Chemistry, Earth Science, Life Science, Physical Science, Physics, Foreign Language, Career Education Courses, Discrete Mathematics, Algebra, Geometry, Calculus, Trigonometry, Probability and Statistics, Art History, Art Appreciation, Music, Online Courses, Physical Education, Health, ROTC
Goal	To reduce the amount of study material to the twenty most important things that might be on a test
Materials needed	All materials that you need to study for a test, a few 4x6 index cards, paper, pencil or pen
Student comments	*"It's hard to only choose twenty important things when studying for a test because everything seems important. It took me a lot of time to get my list down to 20 but as I was doing this, I realized I was learning a lot."*
Instructor comments	*"Some information is obviously going to be more important that others and some material more than other material will more likely be on a test."*
Individual or group	Begins as an individual project and then shared with the group
Lesson duration	50-60 minutes
Finished product to be graded	Submit a copy of your "Twenty Most Important Things".

Why do I need to learn this?

As students spend time trying to select "The Twenty Most Important Things", they are learning the material. In a way, this is what many teachers do when making tests.

Getting Ready for the Activity

1. Two to three days before a test, gather the notes, handouts, and textbook.

The Activity

2. Read through and put a mark next to a term, concept, name, date and anything else that is important and that might be on a test.
3. Refer to everything that is marked and try to reduce all the marked items until there are only twenty of the most important things.
4. Review these twenty items. Share your list with a classmate's list.

Home Learning

When studying for a comprehensive test that has 4-5 chapters, you may want to use "The Twenty Most Important Things" in each chapter.

-ᗝ-Learning Hint

If students have difficulty reducing the information to "The Twenty Most Important Things", encourage them to use comprehensive question prompts such as *discuss, explain, examine, paraphrase,* and *develop.*

27 | Two Minutes, Two Things

Course	U.S History, U.S. Government, World , History / Civilization, Economics, Biology, Chemistry, Earth Science, Life Science, Physical Science, Physics Foreign Language, Career Education Courses, Discrete Mathematics, Algebra Geometry, Calculus, Trigonometry, Probability and Statistics, Art History, Art Appreciation, Music, Band, Online Courses, Career Education Courses, Physical Education, Health, ROTC
Goal	To monitor reading comprehension by selecting the most important information after a two minute reading.
Materials needed	Textbook, timer, paper, pencil or pen
Student comments	*"I never liked reading because it was so boring. This strategy is OK because it's easy to read for two minutes."*
Instructor comments	*"I like this because the whole class does it at the same time. It works well in classes that have a wide range of reading abilities."*
Individual or group	Begins as an individual project and then shared with the group
Lesson duration	20-30 minutes
Finished product to be graded	Submit at least 6 "things" or facts that you read about.

Why do I need to learn this?

This strategy is excellent for all students--those with attention and concentration problems, students who dislike reading and also with strong, capable readers.

Getting Ready for the Activity

1. Select a textbook chapter that students will need to read for upcoming test.
2. Have every student write the name of the chapter and page number on a sheet of paper.

The Activity

3. Give these directions. "When I say, 'begin' start reading the chapter on page X. After you have read for 2 minutes, I will say 'stop'".
4. On your paper take 3 minutes to write two "things" or facts about what you just read that you think are important.
5. At the end of 3 minutes, repeat steps 3-4 at least four times.
6. Review by having students "share" the 'important things' they wrote from the chapter.

Home Learning

This strategy can be used in all content courses. The time may gradually be extended from two to ten minutes.

-🔅-**Learning Hint**

"Two Minutes, Two Things" is a great way to get reluctant readers to begin reading a chapter. With practice students will begin noticing an improvement in reading rate.

28 | VCT: Visual Text Connection

Course	U.S History, U.S. Government, World , History/ Civilization, Economics, Biology, Chemistry, Earth Science, Life Science, Physical Science, Physics, Foreign Language, Career Education Courses, Art History, Art Appreciation, Online Courses, Health
Goal	To connect visual information with the textual information
Materials needed	Textbook and other reference material that has visual information, colored pencil or pen
Student comments	*"I never used to look at the visual material. Now I've learned that connecting the visuals with the written explanation makes everything so easy."*
Instructor comments	*"Many students never look at a drawing, chart, illustration, map, or other visual aide. The visual aides are there to clarify the written text. This is an excellent strategy!"*
Individual or group	Begins as an individual project but results can be shared with group
Lesson duration	10-15 minutes per visual illustration
Finished product to be graded	With your textbook show your instructor how you connected the visual/graphic with the written information.

Why do I need to learn this?

VTC is a study strategy that significantly enhances learning visual/graphic information by "connecting" the visual/graphic to the written information. Most textbooks have diagrams and accompanying explanations---to maximize learning they should be studied together.

Getting Ready for the Activity

1. Identify at least 3 visual/graphics you want to learn about.
2. Find corresponding information from the text which explains each visual.

The Activity

3. Connect the written information from the text for each visual/graphic in the text by drawing a line from the text to the visual/graphic.
4. When reviewing, study both the visual/graphic and the connecting explanation from the text.

Home Learning

Continue this strategy for all visual/graphic illustrations in the text that must be mastered. Review and study the information by looking at the section of the visual and then following the line to the written explanation. Test yourself by making sure you can reproduce and explain all parts of the visual/graphic from memory.

Learning Hint

When reading and studying text, always pause to view the visual/graphic illustration that accompanies the written information. This will help you remember and understand.

---

29 | Wallpaper

Course	U.S History, U.S. Government, World , History / Civilization, Economics, Biology, Chemistry, Life Science, Physics, Earth Science, Physical Science, Foreign Language, Discreet Mathematics, Algebra, Geometry, Calculus, Trigonometry, Probability and Statistics, Foreign Language, Online Courses
Goal	To memorize material for an upcoming test
Materials needed	All materials that need to be mastered for a test, different colored paper, scissors, tape, pencil or pen
Student comments	*"I 'decorated' my room about five days before the test. I kept looking at the little pieces of paper that were all over the room at least eight times a day. It's no wonder that I did very, very well on the test!"*
Instructor comments	*"Sometimes it takes 10-12 times to memorize something. This strategy is excellent. The students don't realize they are studying!"*
Individual or group	Individual
Lesson duration	1-2 hours to make "wallpaper"
Finished product to be graded	Take a picture of your room which you have "decorated" with "Wallpaper"

Why do I need to learn this?

Students who have difficulty remembering terms, formulas, vocabulary, and other facts they need to memorize will enjoy the "Wallpaper Strategy". Students create wallpaper by writing the meaning of the terms, formulas, vocabulary, and facts on colored paper that has been cut into squares, circles, rectangles, triangles, and other shapes. Each of these shapes are taped to the walls, mirrors, and other places where they can easily be seen.

Getting Ready for the Activity

1. Make pieces of "wallpaper" by cutting squares, circles, rectangles, triangles, and other shapes from colored and white paper at least 5 days before the test.

The Activity

2. Write a term, formula, vocabulary word, or fact and the meaning on one of the wallpaper pieces. Use different colored pens to make your wallpaper colorful and vivid.
3. Tape each "wallpaper piece" all over the room.
4. Review by looking at the "wallpaper" every time you enter the room.
5. Take pictures of your newly wallpapered room!

Home Learning

Do the "wallpaper strategy" before every major test. When you are confident you know a term, fact, or vocabulary, remove that piece of wallpaper. On the day of the test, remove all your wallpaper.

Learning Hint

Students will be learning as they make these wallpaper shapes. Memorizing the meaning will be effortless because they "cannot help" but see the shapes many times a day over a 4-5 day period.

30 | Whiz Kid

Course	U.S History, U.S. Government, World , History/ Civilization, Economics, Biology, Chemistry, Earth Science, Life Science, Physical Science, Physics, Foreign Language, Art History, Art Appreciation
Goal	To build comprehension through cooperative learning
Materials needed	Four to five different reading selections based on a different aspect of the topic, paper, pencil or pen
Student comments	*"I like the chance to be an 'expert' and I like teaching my classmates."*
Instructor comments	*"A feature I really like about 'Whiz Kid' is that it builds communication skills. At first the students wanted to read from the selection —now I allow them to put some information on an index card. This gives them a little confidence. Now I see improvement in self-confidence, reading comprehension, and speaking."*
Individual or Group	Group
Lesson duration	One class period
Finished product to be graded	Submit note cards which the "specialist" used to teach members of the home group.

Why do I need to learn this?

"Whiz Kid" builds comprehension within a group. Each member of the group becomes a specialist in one aspect of the topic. After the "specialist" meets with the "specialists" from the other groups, he/she teaches the material to their home group. "Whiz Kid's" features are cooperative learning with small groups and reading comprehension improvement.

Getting Ready for the Activity

1. The teacher prepares 4-5 different reading selections based on topic
2. The teacher arranges students into 4-5 groups. (Ideally, 3-4 students per home group)

The Activity

3. The teacher distributes a different reading selection and 20 note cards to each member of each group.
4. Students with the same selection leave their home group and join the other students who have the same selection as they have.
5. Each member of "specialist" group silently reads his/her selection for approximately 10-15 minutes.
6. After reading silently, the "specialist" group members discuss, share information, and take notes about their selection. This usually takes about 15 minutes.
7. Each group member returns to his/her home group. Each "specialist" takes about 3-5 minutes to teach the information from his/her selection.

Home Learning

Ask students to suggest topics they would like to know more about.

Learning Hint

Try to find articles on the same topic with different point of view--this is a great critical thinking activity.

Three Bonus Strategies: Strengthen reading ability in Math, Science, and History

In the early 1940's, the United States needed to train military personnel in a short amount of time in an effort to win WWII. Dr. Francis Robinson, a professor at Ohio State, realizing intensive training in reading was needed developed SQ3R, the study strategy designed for greater comprehension and retention of textbook material.

SQ3R is a 5-Step systematic study strategy that has been widely used in over 50 years. Some educators called it "the reading formula that helped win WW11."

We have developed three variations of SQ3R and have included them as "bonus strategies". They address the textbook reading challenges found in Math, Science, and History. These classes are very difficult for most people and part of the reason why is because the text is often written at an advanced level and can be extremely complex to read.

The "bonus strategies" are SQ3R Modified for Math, SQ3R Modified for Science, and SQ3R Modified for Historical Sciences. The steps in SQ3R: Survey, Question, Read, Recite, and Review guide the reader toward better understanding and retention. We feel assured that with practice using these bonus strategies, students will become more confident about their progress in math, science and history classes.

SQ3R Modified for Math

Overview: College Math classes are very difficult for most people. Part of the reason why is that the text can be extremely complex to read. By using the SQ3R reading strategy modified for mathematics, you can read through and learn your mathematics text more efficiently. Also, using this strategy will help you understand and remember the information better. When you practice and use SQ3R you will become more confident about your math ability and be able to attain better grades.

Here are the steps for this Strategy:

Survey

Question

Read

Study the Problems

Recite

Review

70

SQ3R Modified for Math

Survey

What to do during this step:

Preview what the chapter is about by:

- ▶ Reading the introduction and conclusion
- ▶ Reading any questions provided by the author-- usually at beginning or end
- ▶ Look at the problems at the end of the chapter
- ▶ Identify and look up any new terms or theorems
- ▶ Review any previously learned terms or equations that you might need to know

Why this step is so important:

When you survey the chapter you are familiarizing yourself with the content and style of the author. You will be better prepared to learn your mathematics information. You will also gain insight into how the sections of the chapter fit together, thereby making it easier for you to understand the math applications necessary.

Practice it!

Open your math textbook to the chapter that you must read for homework. Follow the steps above, paying careful attention to the structure of the chapter. Use the space below to identify any unknown terms and look them up in the glossary.

_____

_____

_____

_____

_____

_____

_____

Now you are ready for the next step, Question...

Question

<u>What to do during this step:</u>

After you have surveyed the chapter, and using what you have learned from class, you should be able to formulate some questions about the reading. Maybe it is something that you are confused about, or something that you are curious to see how a certain problem is solved.

> ▶ You should use the introduction, conclusion, any other chapter sections, and/or class notes to help you develop some questions about the chapter.

<u>Why this step is so important:</u>

When you formulate questions about a topic, you are automatically going to be stimulated to answer those questions. We, by nature, are curious beings. This question and answer technique will help you focus on the topic, helping you maintain concentration and learn better.

<u>Practice it!</u>

Open again to the chapter assigned to you to read. Briefly skim through the first section of the chapter and develop a question that you would like to know the answer to (and you think will be answered in that section). After you have generated a couple of questions for the first section, you will read to answer those questions. Use the bottom of this page to list your questions for the different sections of the chapter.

1._____

2._____

3._____

4._____

5._____

6._____

7._____

8._____

Let's move to the important part, to Read!

SQ3R Modified for Math

Read

What to do during this step:

This step is used in conjunction with the previous Question step. By breaking the chapter into parts by asking questions and reading to find the answers, you are actively reading. So, by this stage you should already:

- ▶ Know what all the vocabulary and symbols mean
- ▶ Have formulated questions for the section you are about to read

Read to answer those questions. Write the answers down. After you have read the entire section, you may want to jot down other notes, ideas or questions that you may have. And do not forget to read each sample problem.

Why this step is so important:

You are now learning how to read **actively**! You are taking responsibility for your own learning by staying focused and concentrating on important pieces of information. Also, it is vital that you read actively in math, especially to do well in the next step, Study the Problems.

Practice it!

Look back to the questions that you created for the first section. Read the section carefully, paying close attention to answering that question and also for any other main ideas that may come up. Use the space below to write the answers to your questions and any other important facts.

1._____
2._____
3._____
4._____
5._____
6._____
7._____
8._____

On to the hard part, Study the Problems...

Study the Problems

<u>What to do during this step:</u>

You are now ready to Study the Problems. This is the hard part for most people. But you should feel confident: You know the vocabulary terms and symbols and have read actively throughout the chapter. So, here's what to do next:

- ▶ Look back to the problems presented in the text
- ▶ Analyze it, putting abstract formulas in your own words
- ▶ Ask yourself these questions:
    - ◆What concepts, formulas, and rules were applied?
    - ◆What methods were used to solve the problem? Why was that method used?
    - ◆What was the first step? Second step? And so on...
    - ◆Have any steps been combined?
    - ◆What differences or similarities are there between examples in the book and any homework problems?
- ▶ Draw diagrams, and use labels

> **Remember-** Take notes and write things in your own words as much as possible. This step will take a while, but it is well worth the effort!

<u>Why this step is so important:</u>

This is probably the **most critical part of reading Mathematics** material, and actually learning from it! This is what the majority of your class lectures will be about, and I would guess most of your test questions will be about too. When you can think about each problem, analyze it, and put it into your own words, you will have made it in Math class!

<u>Practice it!</u>

Use the bottom space to redo the sample problems presented in the section. Keep in mind the questions provided above. Do not look at the book. Use the book only to check your answers.

_____
_____
_____
_____
_____

SQ3R Modified for Math

Recite

What to do during this step:

Go over what you have just done with the problems, and verbalize ,verbalize, verbalize! Putting problem solving into your own words will help you remember what to do on different problems. Focus on the processes used, not specifically the answer. Ask yourself these questions:

- ◆What concepts, formulas, and rules did I apply to solve the problem?
- ◆What methods did I use?
- ◆How did I begin? Walk yourself through the problems again out loud.
- ◆Can I do this problem another way? Can I simplify it?
- ◆Does this problem compare with others from class or homework?

Talk out the problems and then write down your explanations in your notes.

> A good tip-- after studying the problem, close the book and do it yourself.

Why this step is so important:

This is the only way to really learn your mathematics material. You will be much better prepared for classes and for your exams. When you talk things through in your own words, you are stamping that information into your mind. This step will help you remember how to solve math problems so that you don't forget.

Look back at the problem you studied in the last step. Talk out the steps and processes in your own words. Jot down any added information that you may need to. Do not move on to another problem until you are confident that you understand the one you are working on. Use the space below for any notes, or diagrams you want to draw.

Review

What to do during this step:

After about 1-2 days
- ▶ Look back over your chapter and your notes
- ▶ Recite again how you solved each problem
- ▶ Review the vocabulary terms, symbols and formulas
- ▶ List and study the concepts and formulas that are the most important from this chapter

You may need to review multiple times before the next class, or next test. This step should be the easiest because you were actively learning the material along the way.

> You may want to practice additional problems to test yourself to see how well you know the material.

Why this step is so important:

This is the step that will solidify your learning of the material. We all learn by repetition. Reviewing the material will help you learn better and get better grades.

Practice it!

Take some time to review the chapter, problems and your notes. This should be done within about a day or so of completing the Recite stage. Plan ahead so you have multiple times to review, not just cramming the night before the test.

Congratulations! You are well on your way to better understanding and better grades in your Mathematics classes. You have worked hard, and I know you will find the effort pays off!

Worksheet for Examining Returned Math Test

Category	Test Item Missed									# of Items Missed
Preparation	I did not review my notes before the test									
	I did not review my textbook before the test									
	I did not review my old tests									
	I did not make a pre-test to study from									
	I did not partcipate in a study group									
	I did not know how to use my calculator									
Misread directions	I read but did not understand the directions									
	I did not follow all the directions									
Careless error	I put the wrong sign in the answer									
	I had the correct answer but wrote it incorrectly									
	I made a mistake in add./sub./mult./div.									
	I did not do the memory data dump									
	I did not preview the test									
	I did not know how to do the math problem									
	I did not do the second memory data dump									
Test-taking error	I did not set a time limit for each question									
	I did not check for easy questions									
	I spent too much time on one question									
	I left the question blank									
	I skipped the question and didn't go back to review									
	I did not use all of my test time									
Other										

SQ3R Modified for Science

SQ3R Modified for Science

Overview: Reading in the Sciences is one of the most difficult areas for students. With the plentitude of facts, ideas, visual aids and things to understand, it is no wonder that so many students require some extra help. By using this modified SQ3R method, a student in the Sciences can learn how to connect what they read to the visuals that the textbook provides. Also, it teaches students how to think on a higher level in order to really learn the material that is assigned.

Here are the steps in this method:

Survey

Visuals

Read

Question

Review

SQ3R Modified for Science

Survey

What to do during this step:

Look over your chapter for a few minutes to get yourself ready to study it in greater depth. Here are the things you should do before starting the chapter:

- ▶ Read the Title
- ▶ Read the Introduction
- ▶ Read the Headings and bold-typed words
- ▶ Look over the Visuals
- ▶ Read the Summary (if there is none, read the last couple of sentences under each heading)

Get a feel for how the chapter is organzied; it will tell you how the author wants you to learn all of the information. This step should take you about 5 minutes or so.

Why this step is so important:

You are making yourself ready to learn this material. By surveying the chapter you are getting a feeling for what the "Big Picture" is. It is showing how all of the small pieces (signified by headings) fit into the larger scheme (chapter title). So when you actually read the chapter, you will be prepared and start to see connections.

Practice it!

Open your textbook up to the chapter that is assigned to you. Look over the things listed above and then survey the chapter. Start to think about what you are about to read. Make questions in your head about it. Get a feel for how the author organized all of the information.

Visuals

Look at and read the visual(s) on the page first. Make sure that you understand
- ▶ the names of all parts,
- ▶ their functions
- ▶ and/or the sequence of events

as described by the visual only. Gather as much information that you can from the visual, without going into the text.

Next, recite the names, functions or sequence aloud. Then cover the visual with a piece of paper or your hand. See how much you can remember on your own. Then read the visual one more time.

Why this step is so important:

Visuals are a major part of science texts. They can serve as summaries to what the text is about. If you understand the visual, you have a greater chance of understanding the text that you are about to read. Again, you are getting your brain ready to absorb all of this information. Also, when you understand the visuals, it may make reviewing before a test easier for you.

Practice it!

Look at the first visual in your chapter. Using the steps discussed, go ahead and read and review the visual. Use the space below to draw it and write the parts/ functions in your own words.

SQ3R Modified for Science

Read

<u>**What to do during this step:**</u>

Begin to read your chapter, ***one section at a time***. Think about what you are reading and how it relates to the visual or to the Big Picture.

As you read about parts of the visual,
▶ underline each part and draw a line pointing to the section of the visual being discussed.

Another effective method is to
▶ color-code the visual, using different colors for each part, and highlight the text about that part using the matching color.

If there is no visual for your section, read the section and highlight or take notes about the important ideas. Try to create your own visual for the information.

<u>**Why this step is so important:**</u>

By linking what you are reading to the visual you are creating connections in your mind. Now, not only will you remember the text but the picture that goes along with it. When it comes to test time, you will be able to recall the picture, and therefore recall the information. And it will make it easier for you when you are studying this material again.

> The most important thing: Make sure you understand this section <u>before</u> moving on!

<u>**Practice it!**</u>

Read the first section of your chapter. Link the information to the visual, or draw your own visual to link it to. Think about the information, cover the visual again, and try to recall all the information about each part/function.

Question

What to do during this step:

Take the information that you are reading about, or the visual and its' parts, and develop questions about it. Take the time to think of higher level/critical thinking type questions.

For example, if you are studying the sections of the brain, some of your questions might be: What are the functions of this section of the brain? How does this section affect the total brain? What happens if this section is damaged? Etc...

Why this step is so important:

These are questions that you will probably have on your next test. Generally, teachers will ask more higher level questions where you must explain things and make connections, rather than just questions that you can memorize the answers.

If you take the time to do this now, you will learn the material better now and be more prepared for your exams later.

Practice it!

Use the space below for your questions. Remember: Try to think of higher level questions. Pretend you are the professor, what would you ask on an exam?

_____

_____

_____

_____

_____

> Now, here's the catch: *Can you answer <u>every one</u> of these?* If not, go back into the chapter and find out the answers before moving on...

SQ3R Modified for Science

Review

What to do during this step:

Go back and look through the material. Read over your notes, and look again at all of the visuals. This should be done within a day or so of completing the previous steps.

> ▶ Test yourself to see if you can still answer the questions that you created for each section
> ▶ Test yourself to see if you can identify all the sections of the visuals (cover and check)

Again, do this reviewing one section at a time. Once you feel confident about the section, move on to the next. Work your way, in order, through the whole chapter. Think again about the Big Picture and make sure that you understand how all the parts of the chapter fit together.

Why this step is so important:

Reviewing helps cement the material in your mind. The more that we review, the more that we remember. After all of the work you have done in the first 4 steps, this last one should be easy. After a while, you will find that you will be able to review the material faster, because you have learned it during the beginning steps. It is important to remember to give yourself enough time to review before the test, and not to cram the night before.

Practice it!

Within the next day or so, go over the material again. Follow the steps above to review all of it. You will see that your confidence in what you have learned has improved greatly!

Congratulations! You are taking steps to be a better reader and student. Keep practicing this method and you will soon see noticeable improvement!

SQ3R Modified for Historical Sciences

Overview: This reading strategy will facilitate better understanding of Historical Sciences reading material. Combined with this strategy is the use of a Reading Grid, which aides with organization of important facts and ideas. Using this strategy will help you learn more effectively, interpret others' opinions and formulate your own opinions. Better grades are just one of the added benefits of practicing the modified SQ3R.

Here are the steps in the Modified SQ3R strategy:

Survey

Question

Read

Recite/Grid

Review

SQ3R Modified for Historical Sciences

Survey
What to do during this step:

Get to know your textbook and chapter:
- ▶ Read the Introduction and/or Preface
- ▶ Read the headings and bold-type words
- ▶ What is the author's background?
- ▶ What is the author's political orientation?
- ▶ How is the textbook organized?
- ▶ What study aids does your chapter provide?
- ▶ Read the Conclusion of the chapter, if applicable

Start to think about what you are about to read
- ▶ Make predictions
- ▶ Look up any unfamiliar words or vocabulary

Why this step is so important:

You are getting ready to read. When you survey the chapter you are familiarizing yourself with the content and style of the author. You will be better prepared to learn your historical information. You will also gain insight into how the sections of the chapter fit together, thereby making it easier for you to understand the historical themes that arise.

Practice it!

Open your history textbook or material to the chapter that you must read for homework. Follow the steps above, paying careful attention to the structure of the chapter. Use the space below to identify any unknown terms and look them up in the glossary.

_____

_____

_____

_____

_____

Now you are ready for the next step, Question...

Question

<u>What to do during this step:</u>

This step is just like the Question Step in SQ3R that you learned about. Taking one section at a time, you formulate questions that
> ▶ You think will be answered in that section
> ▶ Or that you are curious about, specifically related to that section's topic

Write the questions down for each section. Then read to find out the answers (next Step).

> A good tip-- use the headings to guide your questions, or read the topic sentence and use that to get ideas for questions...

<u>Why this step is so important:</u>

By breaking the reading up into sections, the assignment becomes less overwhelming. Also, by finding the answers to your questions you are maintaining focus and concentration on your reading. Critical readers are constantly questioning and reading to find out the answers. By doing so, you can also weed out the non-important information and retain the important information.

<u>Practice it!</u>

Open up your book or get out an article that you have to read for an assignment. Look at the first section of it and read the heading and/or topic sentence(s). Generate a few questions that you think are important and also that may be answered after reading that section. It should take only a minute or two to generate the questions-- some may be very straightforward, and others should be a bit deeper in meaning.

Use the lines below to write the questions down.

1._____

2._____

3._____

4._____

Now you are ready to Read...   86

SQ3R Modified for Historical Sciences

Read

What to do during this step:

Here is where you will read the first section, thinking about those questions you just wrote. You are reading to find out:
- ▶ The main idea of that section
- ▶ The answers to your questions
- ▶ Any other important facts/ideas you find

> Remember--<u>Read one section at a time</u>. Stop after each one, thinking about the answers to your questions and jotting down any other important ideas.

Why this step is so important:

Reading in sections helps your brain process the information. You are not overwhelmed with information because you are breaking it down into smaller parts. Also, by looking for specific answers to your questions you will understand the important ideas and remember them better, too.

Practice it!

Read the first section of your chapter or article. Keep in mind those questions. Use the space below to write down the answers and any other important ideas that you read in that section.

1._____

2._____

3._____

4._____

_____

_____

_____

_____

Recite

What to do during this step:

After you have surveyed, questioned and read the section, now it is time for you to:
Recall out loud what the main points of that section are
Recall out loud what the answers to your questions are
Recall out loud any supporting details or evidence that you read

In your own words!

Seeing any repetitions here?

Why this step is so important:

Recalling or reciting out loud is important because it forces you to stop and think about what you just read. By saying things out loud to yourself you are helping your mind remember the information.

Grid

After you have verbalizied the information, you should write it down. This will help you when it is time to study or review this material again. Also, by saying and writing it there is a better chance of you remembering it.

Again, you write this down after you have read and recited one section. Then when you feel confident that you understand the main points, you can move on to next section of your assignment. This may seem tedious at first, but it will get easier and quicker with practice.

Practice it!

After reading the first section, recall out loud what the main points are, the answers to your questions and any other details from that section. Then use the Reading Grid provided and write down those same ideas/facts. Only then can you move on to the next section-- and complete the same steps for that section, and so on.

SQ3R Modified for Historical Sciences

Review

What to do during this step:

It is important to review your material soon after you have completed all of these steps.

- ▶ Give yourself about a day or two and then review all of the material
- ▶ You could survey the chapter again
- ▶ Then read your notes, including your questions and answers and your reading grid(s).

Why this step is so important:

Repetition is one of the keys to learning. By reviewing the material again (and again) you are moving that information from your short term memory to long term. You should plan ahead so you do not have to cram before an exam. Give yourself time to review, think about, re-teach yourself, or extend what you already have. By doing so, your understnading of this topic will increase and you will remember the information for a long time.

Practice it!

Reviewing your material could take from about 10 minutes to ???, depending on how well you are understanding the material and remembering it. Hopefully by using the SQ3R strategy, your review time will be on the short side because you have been actively reading, thinking and studying the material along the way. But sometimes the material is more complex and we need more time to review it. You may need to review some sections but not all, depending on your level of understanding. Review one section at a time, like we have been doing, and don't move on until you understand it fully.

<u>Congratulations!</u> When you practice all of these steps, you will notice that your understanding increases and also your grades will improve. These are skills that you will use for the rest of your lives! Keep up the hard work, and it will pay off!

About
the Authors

Patsy Trand, Ph.D., is a faculty member of Florida
International University and the former administrator
of the FIU Reading and Learning Lab. Dr. Trand teaches
undergraduate, honors, and graduate courses for the FIU
School of Arts and Sciences. She is committed to passing
on her wealth of knowledge and experience to help high
school and college students reach their academic goals.
She has authored many articles and has presented at many
national and international conferences.

Kay Lopate, Ph.D., is a Professor Emeritus from the
University of Miami, Miami, Florida where she co-
founded the Reading and Study Skills Center and taught
for the School of Education. Her special interests are
preparing PreMed students for medical school and helping
undergraduates acquire advanced reading ability to
succeed in the demands of mastering college level texts.

Dear Students,

In our long careers as professors at two major universities we have always come to the same two conclusions:

A college education is based on reading

and

Students with high levels of reading
comprehension performed well in their classes
and went on to earn their college degree.

"The 30 Awesome Reading and Learning Strategies for High School Students", based on our conclusions, is the collection of reading and learning strategies that we have developed and used with undergraduate and graduate students. In working with our students we have always emphasized that
"It doesn't matter what your reading level is now—what
matters is what your reading level can become."

We believe that "The 30 Awesome Reading and Learning Strategies for High School Students" will be a key factor that will help you **"become the student you aspire to become".**

We hope you enjoyed the book and begin to use the strategies.
We wish you the best as you continue to reach
your educational goals,
Kay Lopate, Ph.D. and Patsy Trand, Ph.D.

www.ingramcontent.com/pod-product-compliance
Lightning Source LLC
Chambersburg PA
CBHW062049090426
42740CB00016B/3076